# Puberty Pe

## and all that s

## GIRLS ONLY!

## HOW WILL YOU CHANGE?

**Kaz Campbell and Katrina Kahler**

# Table of Contents

# INTRODUCTION

Welcome to our book on Puberty. Get a glass of your favorite beverage, sit back in your favorite chair, and get comfortable. There is a lot of information here, and hopefully you will find all of it very helpful.

There might be parts of this book you want to share with your friends – by all means, do that! Discussing the information here is important and encouraged. Some parts of this book are for girls, others for boys and some parts will help both girls and boys.

If you feel like talking to your parents about anything you read in here, they would surely welcome the chance to discuss it with you. Keeping the lines of communication open is very important, especially during this period of enormous change in your life.

These years are going to be some of the best you'll ever have. The more you understand about your body, your life and the changes you are going to face, the better you will know how to deal with them. Knowledge is power! The more knowledge you have, the smoother the sailing will be.

So let's get started…

# Part 1 - Advice to Girls

## Confidence

When your body is going through so many changes, your confidence can take a hit. You're worried about all sorts of things, from how to handle your period when it starts, to whether your body odor is controlled well enough, to what to do about that cute boy down the street who wants you to be your boyfriend. If it's not one thing at this point, it's another!

Is it any surprise that you are unsure of yourself sometimes?

The cool thing about confidence is that it has to be learned. It's not a natural thing! You have to take the time to build your self-esteem. Those building blocks will eventually bring you to a place of strong confidence, where you feel ready to tackle the world – and win!

In order to become more confident about yourself, take a hard look at your life so far. What have you achieved? What are you proud of? What about you do other people like? What do YOU like about yourself? What are the things that stand out about you? You might have an incredible talent that everyone envies. You might have good grades in your class. Maybe you're great at working with your hands, and you are creative. Perhaps you're the one who always listens, and many of your friends come to you because they know you will be there for them.

There are so many things you can be confident about! Think about what those things are. Then consider what makes you so good at those things. Maybe you have developed that musical talent through many hours of lessons…that means you're persistent. Maybe you're the best listener because you really, truly care about people. Perhaps those great grades are the result of lots of studying, and you can now zip through tests like they're nothing.

How can your skills help others? If you've got the grades, perhaps you could be a tutor and help others bring their grades up, too. Maybe your musical ability is something that a younger student would love to have – why not teach them how to play something, too?

Set goals for yourself. Start with the things you know you are good at, and work from there. Let's talk about music again. If you're really good at playing guitar, why not try playing the drums, too? Perhaps the piano would work well for you. Expand your horizons and test yourself, setting small goals along the way, until your confidence has grown enough to tackle something even bigger.

Another very important part of building confidence is to accept how good you are at something. Many people simply cannot accept a compliment or a "thank you," because they feel as though they have not earned it. Don't fall into that trap! If you have done something to be proud of, then you should be accepting of the praise as well. You've earned it!

Building confidence takes time, but if you start with small goals and work your way up, you will soon find out where your strengths lie – and knowing that will lead you to even more confidence.

## Kicking the Shyness

Everyone gets shy at one time or another. It can be even worse when you are learning to relate to boys in a different way, now that you are all growing up and becoming young adults. Though you might not be able to get over your shyness entirely – most people never do! – you can find good ways to work through it. You'll be glad you did!

Here are some ways to kick the shyness and become more outgoing.

If you're trying to talk to someone new but you don't know how to break the ice, find something you have in common with that person and use it as a conversation starter. Are you in the same math class? Ask a question, perhaps about when a certain assignment is due. That gets you talking, and then you can move on to something else, like how they liked the school assembly last week.

Is there someone you want to talk to, but you seem to clam up every time they come near you? Think about what you want to say to that person. Write it down to get your thoughts in order. Then rehearse it! Say it in front of the mirror with a smile. Do it over and over until you feel comfortable with the words. When you get a chance to talk to that person again, use the words you have rehearsed to open up the conversation. Everything will be easier from that point.

Let one of your friends introduce you. If you have a friend who is much more outgoing than you are, ask them to introduce you to that person who has caught your eye. Be ready to smile, make eye contact, and have something interesting to talk about. In order to figure out how to do all that, go to the paragraph above this one and practice, over and over!

Meet new people through doing things in groups. If there are group activities going on, like a trip to the skating rink or a bunch of people going to the movies, don't be shy and say no...take a chance and say yes! It's much easier to meet people when you are in a big group. You can drop in on conversations and strike up one of your own when you have people of like minds around you.

Most of all, be yourself. Being shy is absolutely okay, and most people have moments when shyness makes them want to hide in a corner. It might take some time to get over your shyness, but by tackling it one situation at a time, you might surprise yourself at how quickly you build the confidence you need to come out of your shell!

## Dealing with the Parents

These next few years can be very difficult on you, but they can be difficult on your parents, too. They are walking down this rocky road with you, and sometimes they are just as lost as you are. You might find that a great relationship with your parents is suddenly on the rocks, and you don't know why. Or the opposite might be true, and your parents might suddenly become your best friends. It's impossible to know how puberty will affect your relationship with your parents, but there are lots of things you can do to make sure that the changes are good ones!

You might find that you are arguing more with your parents than ever before. This is thanks to all the emotion that is flowing through you right now, and especially all the mood swings that have you feeling all out of sorts. Your parents might lose patience with those mood swings, just like you do – and the result can be a flare-up of arguments that don't seem to make any sense.

You might also feel as though your parents don't trust you anymore. Suddenly they are a bit uptight about letting you go to your friend's house. Now they want to know what you are watching at the movies, what your friends are doing, and how you can possibly spend six hours at the mall doing nothing but walking around! They question what you do, and sometimes you could swear they don't trust you at all.

This is a difficult time for your parents, too. For most of your life up to this point, they have known exactly what is going on with you. You've been very available to them and they never really had to wonder where you were or what you were doing. Now that you and your friends are getting older, your parents have to learn to trust you. They remember the pressures of growing up, and they know how serious the challenges can be. They want to know you are safe, but they know they can't keep you with them all the time. So they worry…a lot!

This is why your parents set boundaries for you. They have to learn to trust you and so you have to abide by rules and curfews. It is important that you do the right thing so that you can earn their trust. Those rules might seem a bit extreme at first – after all, why should you have to be home by eight if your friends can stay out until nine? It's only an extra hour!

If you can prove to your parents that you can come home on time, every time, and not complain about their rules, they will be more willing to trust you. The more they trust you, the more freedom they will let you have. It will eventually work out to your favor – but you have to follow their rules to make that happen.

Those boundaries can feel stifling. They can be annoying when it feels like you are the only one of your friends who is at home while everyone else is out at the hottest party of the year. Your parents are trying their best to keep you safe, and they are also trying their best to let you go a little bit. It is going to take time to find a happy medium for all those boundaries.

Sit down with your parents for a discussion about boundaries. Explain to them how you feel, and listen to their side. You might be surprised at just what their fears are! Ask if it is possible to come to a compromise. Instead of saying, "I want to be out with my friends!" try the more understanding approach: "Mom and Dad…what can I do to make you more comfortable with an extended curfew?"

If you approach the situation in a loving, caring manner and stay calm about their answers – even if they are what you don't want to hear – you will earn big points toward more independence. Your parents need to know you are mature, rational, and able to be trusted. Show them, through your actions and your words, that you are willing to abide by their wishes until a compromise can be had.

If you are open with your parents and give them the chance to trust you, you will be surprised at just how great your relationship can become!

## Moods and Feelings

If there is anything for certain in puberty, both for boys and girls, it's the mood swings. You will feel like you are on a rollercoaster of emotion! It's not far from the truth. Your body is releasing hormones all the time now, and it can make you feel a little crazy.

The mood swings during puberty happen for many reasons. Not only are you dealing with a flood of hormones, you are also trying to handle the anxiety that comes along with the process itself. You are probably a little concerned about how you are developing, and of what your friends and family might think. Anxiety can make everything seem so much worse than it really is, and that can lead to major mood swings.

But keep in mind that these mood swings are normal. Look at it this way: You can see many of the changes happening in your body. You can't see what is happening inside, but the changes to your mind are just as strong, if not stronger, than what your physical body is going through.

That puts mood swings into some perspective, doesn't it?

The first way to combat mood swings is to understand them. You know they are coming from the changing hormones, and there is little you can do about that. So be kind to yourself! Recognize that you are going to have mood swings. It's a fact. You can, however, help yourself by doing the following things:

**Talk with someone.** Speaking to someone who has been through the mood swings can help you deal with your own. Talking about the way you feel and having a lot of understanding in return is a perfect way to ease the mood swings and remind you that you really are okay. This is natural – even if it feels that it isn't.

**Ask all the questions you need to ask.** Don't hesitate to ask for reassurance. You really need it right now! Hearing kind words from someone who has been in your position is a sure-fire way to ease the stress of those mood swings and make you feel better about everything that is happening to you right now.

**Keep everything in perspective.** When you feel yourself getting emotional, take a deep breath and think about what is happening. Try to think rationally, not emotionally. It is a hard thing to do, but simply focusing on trying to do it will help you get your emotions under control.

If you need to have a good cry, go do it. If you need to be alone for a while, that's okay too. You might need to take some time out from everyone in order to put things back into perspective. Your good judgment can be clouded by mood swings right now, so take time to think about things before you act.

## Managing Your Anger

Sometimes your mood swings can take the form of anger. This might be the most unsettling thing of all. Getting angry for no reason can make you think as though you have no control over what is happening to you, and that can make you even angrier. Such anger can be frightening and can leave you wondering what is wrong with you. Why can't you just be as cool and calm as you used to be?

Everyone gets angry sometimes. With all the changes you are dealing with right now, it's no wonder you feel like flying off the handle from time to time! Knowing how to handle your anger is what matters.

Pay attention to how you feel. There will usually be something that happens before the anger starts. Are you getting enough sleep? Are you eating healthy foods? Are you spending time outside in the fresh air, exercising as much as you can, and spending time with friends who make you laugh?

If any of these thing are lacking, your odds of getting angry over the tiniest things go up.

When you do get angry, what do you do? Do you throw things? Punch things? Say things that are meant to hurt someone else? If you are very honest with yourself about what you do when you are angry, you can see how destructive some of your actions might be. When you realize you're getting angry, take a step back and remember how much your actions could hurt someone else. Knowing what you are capable of doing when you are angry, and how those things can affect other people, might be enough to calm you down.

If you're angry and you can't seem to shake it, get physical. Exercise! A good, hard run will get your blood pumping and clear your head. If you listen to music while you are going it, great! Music can affect you mood and help you calm down as well.

Another good tip for managing your anger is to keep a journal. Sometimes these are called "slam books" because you can slam your thoughts into them instead of slamming a door! When you write down the things that bother you, it's easy to look back at them when you are in a calmer state of mind and question your reactions. Did you go overboard? Did you really represent the situation clearly and fairly? What started the whole thing, and how could you have changed that?

The most important part of managing anger is taking the time to think about what you are going to say or do. Going with your knee-jerk reaction is almost always making the wrong choice. Instead of yelling at your parents or putting your foot into the door, take deep breaths. Storm off if you have to – remove yourself from the situation. Then take some time to think. Don't let anger get the best of you!

If you are still very angry and you can't fight it off, it's time to talk to someone about it. Go to your guidance counselor, your parents or another trusted adult to discuss the problem.

**Are you Depressed?**

Sometimes your mood swings can be very deep, almost to the point of altering your day-to-day life. You might start to wonder if you're depressed.

Feeling down or sad is very common among young people your age. Depression is sometimes triggered by a major loss or life change, but more often than not, there is no clear explanation for it. You just feel very sad and upset for a long time, and you feel like there is nothing you can do to shake it.

There are specific signs of depression, and they can happen to anyone at any age. Have you experienced any of the following symptoms?

Feeling sad for no reason

Having no energy

Pulling away from friends and family

Avoiding things you used to enjoy, like a cookout with your family or the movie night with your friends

Losing weight – or gaining in

Either sleeping too little or too much

Feeling guilty, worthless, or unappreciated

Indifference, or not caring about the world around you

An achy body but no medical cause for it

Persistent headaches

Inability to concentrate

If you are experiencing these symptoms, you could be facing depression. It's time to talk to someone about this. Go to your parents, your guidance counselor, your coach, or someone else you trust. Tell them you are feeling down, and that you read over a checklist of symptoms and you are wondering if you are depressed. Make it clear that you are very concerned, and they should take you seriously, too.

Unfortunately, some people will not notice if someone around them is depressed. They might chalk it up to laziness, a mood swing or other things that are very different from depression. It can be hard to see someone you care about going through something so difficult, and that is often a reason many parents fail to notice depression in their children.

If you approach someone who doesn't believe you are depressed, it's time to get a second opinion. Visit your doctor and explain the situation. Your doctor can help decide what would be the best course of treatment, and can provide tips for your specific situation that will help you rise out of the depression and feel like your happy self again.

## Stress and Anxiety

Stress might be something you never dreamed could happen to you. That's for people who are older, right? Your parents, for instance. Stress is something that affects them, not you! But you might be surprised just how much pressure and stress young people your age can experience.

It is a well-known fact that big life events, such as seeing your parents go through a divorce or dealing with the death of someone close to you, can bring on major stress. However, you might be surprised by some of the other things that can make you feel incredibly tense and stressed out.

Stress can be brought on by almost anything. If you have shaky grades in a class and test time comes up, that can be enough to stress you out. If you're dealing with a boy or girlwho really likes you and you don't know how to handle it, that can stress you out, too. Even thinking about things like potential colleges, the dance on Saturday night or how your parents will react to your date are all events that can lead to stress. One of the most common causes of stress is having friendship problems. Friends at your age are very important and when things go wrong it can be very hurtful and stressful.

## Exercise Can Really Help

When you are stressed out, the first thing to do is find a natural way to relax. The best way to do that is by engaging in some exercise. Not only is it good for your body, it also helps clear your mind and give you a new perspective on how to deal with the things that are bothering you.

There are some great ways to fit exercise into your daily routine:

Make a point of walking. If you're going to your friend's house down the street, ask your parents if you can walk instead of get a ride from them. Even that short distance will help.

Take the stairs instead of the elevator whenever you are

presented with the choice.

Take up yoga and do your exercises while you are watching your favorite television show.

Find a sport that looks like fun and give it a try! A good round of basketball will get your blood pumping.

## Other Relaxation Tips

There are many other ways you can combat stress. Here are a few tips to get back on an even keel:

Get enough sleep. A good night's sleep will help clear your mind, and that's great to beating stress. If your body is well rested, handling anything will seem much easier.

Eat properly. Eat the right foods! When you stress out, you are likely to do one of two things: You either eat too much, or you don't eat enough. During periods of stress you have to pay close attention to what you are eating. Eat lots of fruits and vegetables, as well as lean meats (like fish or chicken). Drink plenty of water. A balanced diet will help your mood.

Chill out. Give yourself time to just relax. That doesn't mean playing video games or sitting in front of the television. In fact, those activities can lead to even greater stress!

Do something that helps clear your mind, like yoga or writing in a journal. Take a long nature walk, and don't bring along your iPod or other distractions. Just take the time to enjoy something different.

Talk to someone. If you feel more connected with others, your stress level will drop. Having someone on your side that understands what you are going through always helps, so look for someone who has been where you are now. Tell them how you feel and ask them how they handled the same situations. Knowing you are not alone is a huge step toward overcoming a stressful situation.

Breathe deep. That sounds like a cliché, doesn't it? Taking deep breaths or sitting down to meditate might seem like quirky new-age stuff, but guess what? It really does work. Simply sit down somewhere quiet, close your eyes, and concentrate on your breathing. This helps you close out the rest of the world and makes you focus on you, and only you – and it clears your mind so you can think more clearly about the situation you're in.

Think positive. It can be hard to think positive when you are stressed to the max, but it's important to remember that this will pass. Thinking about what life will be like after that stressful moment has gone by will be a great way to stay positive! Something that usually works well is to remind yourself that it could be worse – you could be dealing with something far more drastic than what has been handed to you right now. You can overcome this!

## When is Anxiety a Problem?

Sometimes stress can seem more severe than it should be. If you are constantly worrying about something and can't seem to shake that feeling, you might be experiencing an anxiety disorder. The difference between stress and anxiety is rather simple: Stress eventually goes away, usually when the thing that is stressing you out is over or gone. Anxiety, however, remains no matter what you do to relax.

Anxiety can lessen your quality of life and lead to other problems, such as lack of concentration or irrational fears. This is why anxiety needs to be treated as soon as possible! You don't want to become a slave to worry about things that you can do nothing about, do you?

If you are dealing with an anxiety issue, it's a good idea to see a professional counselor. They can help you pinpoint what is causing the anxiety and give you ways to combat the problem.

## The Pressures of Growing Up

As you begin your journey into adulthood, you will be presented with some very adult situations. You might not feel ready for these things, and you might not know what to do. That's one of the pressures of growing up, and it happens to everyone. How you deal with it makes all the difference.

When you begin to grow and change, your emotions and thoughts begin to change, too. You or your friends might begin to wonder about things that you never thought about before. Sex is a good example – you probably never gave it a passing thought before, but now that puberty has set in, you might be curious.

Your natural curiosity is a good thing, but it should always have rational limits. Those limits are there to keep you safe.

Even the most seasoned adults put limits on their curiosity, and now is the time in your life when you learn how to do that.

When your friends are trying something new, it can be very tempting to you. And believe it or not, that temptation makes perfect sense. Your friends are doing it, and you want to fit in. You see them having fun and you want to have some fun, too.

But what really matters is how you deal with that temptation!

This is your chance to prove to everyone – your friends, your family, and even yourself – of just how mature you can be. If you can look past the temptation and avoid those things that are bad for you, you are one step closer to becoming a responsible adult.

At your age, it isn't unusual to be offered things that make you uncomfortable. If you see someone else smoking a cigarette and they offer you a puff, you have a very big decision to make. You can take that puff and try to "look cool" or fit in with the gang. Or you can put yourself first, think about your health and your reputation, and decline those cigarettes.

It's the same with alcohol or drugs. You already know that alcohol and drugs can hurt your body. These substances can cause changes in your brain chemistry, your body makeup, and your attitude. They can even wind up killing you. The kids who drink alcohol or do drugs and try to convince you it's all right are the ones who will wind up in serious trouble down the road. Do you really want to put yourself in that position?

There are also some kids who think it's cool to "test" themselves by doing dares. Let me tell you a little story:

When I was fourteen, a good friend of mine decided she was going to hang out with the "cool crowd." She began doing things that were completely out of character for her, like sneaking out when her parents told her she couldn't go somewhere, or making out with boys that were much older than her. Eventually she started drinking, and she tried marijuana a few times. By the time we were fifteen, I no longer recognized my old friend.

A few months later, she got arrested for shoplifting. She and her "cool friends" thought it would be fun to see who could steal the most from the shopping center. They all got caught, and they all went to the police station in handcuffs. Nothing will turn your world upside down faster than being arrested!

The moral of the story is this: When you start going down the wrong road, it can be very easy to let things escalate. When my friend decided she wanted to be one of the "cool kids," I'm sure her dreams never included sitting in a jail cell. It's always important to think about your actions and what the consequences could be.

Some kids your age worry about what happens if they do refuse the bad stuff. Will you be laughed at? Ridiculed? Called names? Will you be considered a sissy or a scaredy-cat? Will rumors begin to fly?

This is a very big lesson to learn about rumors, gossip and bullies. We'll talk more about it in the next chapter, but here's what you need to know right now: When someone makes fun of you for not doing what they want you to do, they are trying to bring you down to their level. They feel guilty about what they are doing, and they want someone else to do it with them, so they will feel a bit better about themselves. When you refuse, they realize what they are doing is wrong – and instead of being mature enough to admit it and stop what they are doing, they choose to attack you instead.

When it comes to peer pressure and temptation, prove your maturity and stick to your guns! You don't have to do things that hurt your body just to fit in. You don't have to do anything that makes you uncomfortable. Anyone who tries to convince you otherwise is NOT your friend.

## What if someone pressures you into doing something sexual?

In the midst of all those raging hormones, you're feeling a lot of new things. When you reach your teens one of those new, strong feelings might be sexual desire. This is the time when many girls and boys plunge headfirst into some choices they could regret later. Make sure you aren't one of them by knowing exactly how to treat yourself – and your friend – with the respect you both deserve.

There might come a time in your relationship when your boyfriend or girlfriend brings up the subject of becoming more intimate. He or she might be curious and just want to talk about how you feel. Talking about it is one thing, but feeling pressured in any way is quite another.

If you feel pressured to do anything you don't feel comfortable with or something that you know your parents wouldn't allow you to do, it's time to take a step back and look hard at the situation you're in. You should never, EVER feel pressured to do something that makes you uncomfortable. If you are feeling this way, then something is not right.

Having intimate relationships should be your decision, on your own terms, and it is not something to take lightly. If someone is pressuring you to do things you know you should do or feel funny about, they aren't giving you the respect or consideration you deserve.

Don't buy the "You would if you loved me" line or anything of the sort. If your friend loved you, he or she wouldn't be asking you to do something that made you uncomfortable. If anyone ever uses your emotions to coerce you into something, that speaks volumes about their lack of character. That's not a person who deserves your love.

Some young teens have sex and it can be a life-changing experience, not only for the emotion involved with such an act. Sex can lead to pregnancy, as well as sexually transmitted diseases. A sexual experience is something that stays in your mind forever. Consider carefully what you want your experiences to be like, because you will have to live with those memories for a lifetime! Feeling pressured into something so important and life changing is not a good memory to have.

If your friend continues to pressure you into doing sexual things, it is time to end the relationship.

## If it Ends...

Sometimes relationships just don't work out. When you feel like it's time to go your separate ways, how do you tell your friend? Breaking up is never easy, but there are some ways you can make it easier:

Break up with them in person if at all possible. It might seem harder to do it this way, but it's much better in the long run than simply writing a note or sending a text or an email. Never break up using a Facebook status, that is mean!

Be as gentle as you can. Tell your friend you still care about him or her, and praise them for the good qualities they have. Be willing to spend time listening to what they have to say. Be ready to answer all of their questions.

When they ask you for your reasons, be completely honest. The only thing worse than being broken up with is being lied to in the process. By being honest, you are keeping a level of respect between the two of you. That goes a long way toward healing a broken heart.

Be prepared for the question of whether you can get back together. If you've made up your mind, stick with your decision. Your friend might try to convince you to stay with them, and when they're in front of you with those sad eyes, it might be very tempting to go back on your decision to break up. Remember that you have thought about this long and hard, and you're making the decision that's right for you.

It's never easy to break up with someone, but remember – it's even worse to be the one on the other side of the equation. In fact, there might come a time when a person you really like decides to break up with you.

Rejection can sting. The crushing disappointment, the embarrassment of knowing it didn't work out, and the feeling of failure is a normal reaction. Adults have the same reactions when their relationships end. Don't believe you have to "play it cool" and act like it doesn't affect you. It hurts, it is a loss, and it should be recognized as such.

Take the time to cry. It's okay to think about what might have been, and it's alright to wonder why. If you're lucky, they have told you their reasons. Accept them for what they are, even if you don't agree with them. Part of growing up is accepting that sometimes, people do things that you don't understand.

Take your time to hurt over the breakup – and then take a deep breath, know that broken hearts will heal, and soldier on. Soon you will be having fun again!

**Find out who your friends are!**

When everything about your body seems to be changing, you're not alone. It's happening to all of your friends, too. They are going through just as many changes are you are, and it affects everyone in different ways. Some of your friends might be acting weird, or they might accuse YOU of acting weird. You might find yourself getting closer with other friends who seem to understand you, while you are pulling away from the friends you have known all your life.

It's hard to know who your true friends are. It's even harder to know whom your true friends are when you are in the midst of growing up and you have so many emotions swirling around you.

Your true friends will make themselves known. How? You will know it when you see it. Your true friend is the one who sticks by your side when you're sick and brings you hot soup to drink. True friends are the ones who put aside their own needs and wants and go the extra mile to take care of YOU.

The best of true friends are the ones who stand up for you, no matter what the situation. They are the ones who will be there when you call in the middle of the night, hold you when you break up with your first boyfriend, and make a point of getting to know your parents almost as well as they know you. They are the ones who will be right by your side, crying along with you, when a loved one passes away.

When you are a bit older, true friends are the ones who will drive through snow to get to you and freeze their fingers while they help you change a tire. They are the ones who are always there and never let you down. They are good for those weekend shopping trips, those long nights talking about the things that frighten you, and those serious moments when you don't know what to do. Friends help you through everything.

Making friends can seem daunting. Getting to know someone that well takes time and patience! If you have been talking to someone that you think could become a great friend, make a point of helping that friendship along. Invite your potential new friend to go to the mall with you, or have them over for a study night. If you have lots of things in common, your initial friendship will gradually evolve into a much stronger one.

Sometimes friendships just happen, and when that is the case, it's great! When I was twelve, I met a new friend because I got seated next to her at a play. We talked during the intermission and then exchanged phone numbers. We talked for hours! She became my best friend, and to this day – over twenty years later! – she's still my best friend in the whole world. If a friendship is supposed to blossom, it will.

That doesn't mean that your friendships will always be smooth sailing. You will have times when you argue, and times you don't get along. Arguing with your friend is a very difficult thing, because this is the person you are supposed to be able to talk to about anything! Hurting your friend's feelings also hurts you, because you care about your friends. When they hurt, so do you.

If you do find yourself in an argument with a friend, give yourselves both time to cool off and think about things. It's okay not to talk for a few days. But once the emotion blows over, it's time to make apologies. Talk to your friend about what happened. If it is a situation you need to discuss further, make a point of doing that. Sit down and hash it all out. Always make it clear that you want to get over the argument and you value the friendship!

True friends can work through the problem and come out with an even stronger bond. A good, strong friendship is worth the effort.

## Coping with Bullies

Unfortunately, you also have to learn to deal with the very opposite of a "true friend" – the bully.

Bullying is a very big problem for millions of young people just like you. Anyone who is "picked on" or bothered for any reason is being bullied. Usually bullies will attack things that they know will bother you. If you have acne, a bully is likely to make fun of it. If you are shy or quiet, bullies will tease you about that. If you are the outgoing type, they might even tease you for that, too! Bullies usually pick and choose their victims at random, and they will hammer away at their target until they get a response. If that response is anger or tears, the bully has just won that particular battle.

If their verbal insults don't work, they might even attempt to turn the situation physical by tripping you, yanking on your clothes, knocking your books out of your hands, or doing other things that are not only annoying, but dangerous.

Bullies have discovered the Internet, and now they use that to bully their victims as well. Cyber bullying can take the form of nasty emails, instant messages that make you cringe, or comments posted on public boards that try to tear down your character and reputation.

If the bully keeps it up and there is no end in sight, some victims can begin to feel intense fear. Going to school becomes a dreadful chore. Going out with friends can be nerve-wracking. Even checking email can be frightening.

### How to calmly fight back

The best way to fight a bully is to never give them what they want. They are trying to get a rise out of you – they think that making you cry or making you furious is great entertainment. They watch for reactions, find something that works, and then keep hammering away at that particular weakness.

If the bullying is verbal or psychological, there are specific ways to handle it. Here are some of the things that might help:

**Ignore the bully.** By ignoring the words, you are not giving the bully what he or she wants. Walk away with your head held high and avoid giving any reaction. This is much easier said than done, as walking away is the hardest thing you might have to do. It's certainly MUCH harder than lashing out at the person who is trying to hurt you. Take the high road and show the bully you will not be bothered by the comments.

**Talk to someone about it.** Make your counselor and teachers aware of what is happening. Tell your parents as well. If it is simply verbal abuse from this bully, you can probably handle it on your own, but they need to know so that if it does escalate, you have someone on your side ready to take action.

**Hide the anger.** Don't let the bully see how furious you are. Don't let them control you! Controlling you and your emotions is a bully's dream come true, so don't fall for it. Try to be perfectly calm and collected when a bully is harassing you. You might be furious on the inside, but on the outside, you don't seem to care. Pretend you're going for the Academy Award and ignore the jerk.

**Turn to your real friends.** When the bullies start rumors about you, or when word gets around that someone has it out for you, your true friends are the ones who will stand by you.

**Don't let it get physical.** Remove yourself from the bullying situation as soon as you possibly can. If the bully tries to get physical with you, don't let the situation escalate. If the bully physically attacks you, it's time to go to your parents and your guidance counselor. If it is happening away from school, it's time for you and your parents to go to the authorities. Bullying that turns into physical violence is no longer bullying – it's physical assault, and that is a crime.

## How to handle gossip or rumors

Gossip and rumors can be very hurtful. It hurts to know that someone is talking badly about you behind your back. It hurts even more to know that so many people might believe the lies about you!

Unfortunately, there is very little you can do about rumors or gossip. These comments usually run their course in a day or two, and then the gossipmongers move on to something else. Keeping your cool during those days is the best way to make sure the gossip doesn't get any worse.

Keep in mind that those who spread gossip or start rumors are cowards. They are trying to make themselves look better by pretending they know private and personal information. In reality, they are cowards because they don't have the guts to come face-to-face with you. They want to wreak havoc from their little corner and never actually confront anyone.

You can burst their bubble by confronting the comments. When you hear the rumors about you, nip them in the bud by telling YOUR side of the story. A firm "It's not true" or "I wasn't even there that night – I was at home with my mother" can cut the gossip right where it grows. Your close friends can get into the act by addressing the rumors as well. As soon as they hear someone talking about it, dropping in with the news "I know it's not true, and here's why" can bring those rumors to a screeching halt.

When you do tell your side and the rumors begin to dissipate, the person who started the problem in the first place will be looked upon with suspicion. Obviously, that rumor wasn't true, so is anyone going to trust the next one? The person who begins rumors and spreads gossip is always the one who loses out in the end.

Being the subject of rumors is never a good feeling. So when you hear a rumor floating around, don't pass it along. Nip it in the bud if you can. You're doing a favor for someone who needs it, and you're making yourself feel good by doing the right thing.

One more thing, don't ever gossip or talk negatively about another person. It always gets back to the other person. If you want to be seen as a great person then you should always follow this rule.

You can find more information on how to be popular and make friends easily in our book: How To Win Friends And Influence People for Kids.

## Pimples and Acne

Breakouts. Pimples. Acne! It is one of those things that everyone hates about puberty. You can handle the periods, the mood swings, even the changes in your body shape, but acne is something that everyone dreads. It's easy to see why – acne is usually on your face, where everyone can see it, and it can be difficult to cover up. No wonder so many people see acne as the worst part of their growing-up years!

Let's dispel some myths about acne. First, it is not caused by dirty skin. Acne can happen to someone who has a perfectly clean face and body. Things like chocolate, candies or soda don't cause it. In fact, it isn't caused by anything like that at all.

Acne is caused by the oil glands in your skin. These oil glands are usually good things, and they help keep your skin looking the way it should. But when you go into puberty, those oil glands go a little crazy. Those oil glands release too much oil, and when you combine that with the dead skin cells all of us have on our bodies, inflammation of your pores can occur. That is called acne.

There is no way to predict who will get acne and who won't. If some of your relatives had acne, the odds of you getting it are a bit higher. But even those who have no history of acne in the family could wind up with a bad case of it themselves. You can't even be sure where it's going to happen – some get acne on their face, but others wind up with it on their shoulders, backs or chest. It's thanks to all those hormones going wild – you just never know exactly what is going to happen!

There are ways to combat acne. The easiest way is to wash your face every day. When you wash your face, you are getting rid of the excess oil that has accumulated, as well as washed away those dead skin cells that can lead to acne.

Always wash after exercising. Physical activity can send those oil glands into even higher overdrive! It's always good to shower after the activity, and if you make a facial cleanser part of your routine, it should become an easy thing to remember.

If you are a girl, when you choose makeup, make sure it's the kind that doesn't clog pores. These are often called nonacnegenic or hypoallergenic. When you are at home, wash off the makeup and go natural.

Whatever you do, don't squeeze the pimples to make them go away. It might be tempting to do this, but you could actually make the problem worse. Squeezing a pimple can force the infection further into the skin, leading to even more acne or scarring.

**Other Treatments**

If your acne is getting worse and the basic cleansing options no longer work, it's time to look into over the counter products. There are many products out there that claim to clear up acne, but the only ones that are proven to work are benzyl peroxide and salicylic acid. If you can find a product with both of these ingredients, you're on the road to getting rid of that acne!

Some cases of acne might require a doctor's prescription to clear up. Don't hesitate to talk to your doctor about acne medications. If you do have a prescription for acne medication, be sure to use it exactly as directed.

You might think acne will never go away, but there's good news – it will! Acne will run its course during your growing-up years, and by the time you reach adulthood, all that acne will be a thing of the past. Your body will finish growing and your oil glands will get back under control.

## CONCLUSION

I hope this part of the book has answered some of your questions. You will probably have many more, and that's actually a good thing – the more curious you are, the more you will learn! There are three more sections to this book, one for boys, girls and parents.

If you have further questions about things that are happening to your body and mind at this point in your life, don't hesitate to ask your parents, your doctor or another trusted adult.

# Part 2: Puberty
# How Will I Change?

**Am I Really Normal?**

Believe it or not, this is the question everyone you know is asking about himself or herself. Even those girls who seem so confident about absolutely everything – you know the ones. Even they are looking in the mirror and getting a little nervous about the changes in their bodies and minds.

Puberty can be a really rough time. We're all a little afraid of the unknown, and when that unknown things is happening to YOU, it can be even more frightening. That's why it's so important to learn about what is happening. You're taking a great first step by picking up this book and finding out the answers to what is going on with you!

Everyone has been there at some point in his or her young lives. I've been there, too! When I went through puberty, the changes in my body were so fast and furious; I wasn't sure what would come next. I wasn't even sure what puberty was until I saw a slide show at school about the changes that would occur in my body. I even remember telling my grandmother that I wished there was some magic remedy I could take that would stop time and let me be a carefree little girl forever.

Come on, admit it – you've wished the same thing, haven't you?

My moods were in a tailspin, too. I actually screamed at my

mother once – for no reason at all! – and spent the next week wondering what in the world was wrong with me. I had never done anything like that before, and I couldn't imagine ever doing it again! I couldn't stop apologizing, and I didn't get why she wasn't mad at me. She acted like she completely understood.

Then I started crying at the drop of a hat. Again, for no reason.

I thought I was going crazy.

What was this beast puberty had unleashed in me? Was I doomed to stay this way forever? How did anyone cope with this?

The truth is this: You ARE normal. Your body is doing what it was designed to do.

It might feel weird. It might be embarrassing. It might leave you feeling a little out of sorts, as if this body you're in is suddenly not your own! You might feel like you're losing control of who you are. Believe it or not, all of this "abnormal" stuff really IS normal.

You might not appreciate it all right now, but there will come a day when you will be in awe of the miraculous changes your body goes through to take you from a child to an adult. Even so...it's a hard road to get there, isn't it?

You've done yourself a huge favor by sitting down to read this book. Read it however you like – if there is a particular problem you are having or a big concern on your mind, go straight to that section. But promise yourself that you will read this entire book. At some point, all of the information in here will come in handy for you.

Peace of mind is a beautiful thing to have when you are facing the unknown. Puberty is the unknown for you – so read this book all the way through and feel confident in having that peace of mind!

## Precocious Puberty

What does this mean? Well we don't all go through puberty at the same time. Some girls start to show signs of puberty at a very young age, even as young as 5. But usually precocious puberty in girls happens between the ages of 7 to 10.

It usually starts with: the breasts start to grow and feel sore, underarms hair starts to grow, a growth spurt where the girl gets taller quickly, body odor and sometimes pimples.

Normally these types of signs will happen for a couple of years before the girl gets her first period.

This can be a really hard time for young girls, both physically and emotionally. If this happens to you, don't worry, you are normal and all your friends will eventually go through puberty too.

## What's Going On?

To say your body is changing right now is an understatement. You might feel like there is a whole different person inside you who is trying to come out! In a funny way, you're right. It's the adult version of you that is trying to emerge.

All this craziness actually began a few years ago, though the changes were so subtle you might not have noticed them. You started to grow taller, and your body shape changed just a little. You probably had to buy new clothes, and your parents might have made comments about how you were growing so fast. You didn't know it then, but that was the beginning of puberty!

It was easy back then, wasn't it? What you're facing now seems like a whole new world.

Let's talk about what to expect from this point on. You will probably experience many of these changes. Some of them you have already dealt with, but you might not have understood exactly what it all meant. The following sections will have insight into the crazy way your body and your mind are behaving lately.

## Breasts

When you go through puberty, your breasts will start to grow. At first your chest might be a little achy, or your chest might be ultra-sensitive. Your nipples will gradually get larger, but it might happen so slowly that you don't notice it at first. When your breasts begin to grow, they will start with a small swelling behind your nipple – it's probably not enough for anybody else to notice, but you do! Your shirt will still hide what's happening to your body, so you don't have to worry about anyone else knowing your secret just yet.

### Is it Time for a Bra?

If that question is in the back of your mind, it just might be time to get your first bra. Usually girls need a bra when their breasts become big enough for other people to notice they are growing. Sometimes you will decide you want to wear a bra because the weight of your breasts is a bit uncomfortable, and a bra to hold them up would make life much easier.

### What Type of Bra Do I Need?

There are so many options for bras; you might not know where to start! The most important thing about buying a bra is to remember that fit is important. If a bra doesn't fit properly, it won't be comfortable, and it won't do what it is meant to do, which is support your growing body. It is worth the time to make sure you find a bra that fits you well.

There are some basics to bra size, and these will help you determine which bra is right for you. You can figure all this out with a simple measuring tape!

In order to choose the right bra, you need to know your cup size and your chest size (sometimes your chest size is known as the "band" size). The chest or band is the part of the bra that runs around your body, and usually fastens at the back. The cup size is the size of your breasts themselves. A combination of these two measurements will give you the proper bra size for you.

To get your chest measurement, take the tape measure and place it just under your breasts. Rap it all the way round your rib cage and back. Make sure the tape rests flat on your skin, but don't make it too tight. Now, look at the measurement, and add five inches (13 cm). If the number is odd, round up to the closest even number. There you have it: your chest measurement!

Now, figure out your cup size. You're going to take the measurement of the fullest part of your breasts. Find the fullest part of your breasts (looking in a mirror will really help with this) and measure it just like you did your chest measurement. Write that number down.

Now, subtract your chest measurement from your cup measurement. If the difference between the two numbers is less than one inch (2 cm), your cup size is an AA. If it's one inch (3 cm), you go up to a size A. Two inches (5 cm) equals a B, three inches (8 cm) equals a C, and four inches (10 cm) equals a D.

So let's say your chest measurement is a 34. After you subtract the cup measurement, you get a B cup. That means your bra size is a 34B.

Now you know what to look for at the store!

When you do to try on bras, don't fret if the first one you

attempt doesn't fit properly. Measurement with your tape measure is not an exact science, but it will get you on the right track to which bra works best for you. Remember that each bra will have hooks at the clasp that allow you to adjust the size a bit, as well as sliding adjustments on the shoulder straps. Play with these a bit and see if you can make the bra fit properly with a small adjustment here and there.

If that doesn't work, try a different bra until you find the one that feels right. Your bra should be snug, but shouldn't cut into your skin at all, and it should provide enough lift for your breasts to make you feel comfortable. Often your first bra will be made of soft stretchy material. Don't buy underwire bras; you won't need one of these for a few years at least.

One more note on choosing the proper bra: If you are very active and you're looking for something to keep your breasts from bouncing while you play sports, look into sports bras. These are specially made to keep your breasts comfortable while you are doing something very active. In fact, they can feel so good; some girls might choose to wear a sports bra all the time!

### Dealing with Teasing

When your breasts become bigger and you start wearing a bra, you might be teased by your classmates, especially boys. Unfortunately, this is something almost every girl your age will have to endure. The teasing can be very embarrassing, especially because it brings the changes in your body to the attention of everyone else.

You can keep the upper hand by remembering that everyone goes through the same changes. Even those boys who are teasing you will go through some strange changes of their own in a few years, and they will feel just as uncomfortable as you do now.

The best thing to do about the teasing is to ignore it. Of course, that's very hard to do, and sometimes boys will keep trying until they finally get a response out of you. If you must respond to the teasing, make sure your comments are very calm and sensible. If you lash out at someone who is teasing you about your breasts, they will see that as incentive to tease you even further.

It's hard to do – but ignoring them really is the best option you have.

## Body Hair

Just as your body is starting to grow breasts, other weird changes are happening. You might notice hair growing in places where you hadn't seen any before. You might have always had baby-soft hair on your legs, the kind of hair that is almost invisible – but suddenly that hair is becoming darker and thicker. You will also notice hair under your arms. Even your eyebrows will begin to look bushy!

You will start to see hair in your private areas, too. This is called pubic hair, and it is something everyone gets. It is caused by all those hormones kicking in and trying to take your body into adulthood. It can be very annoying, and you will probably start to wonder how to get rid of it.

## Hair Removal

The good news is this: You don't have to live with all that hair on your body. Millions of people remove hair from their bodies every single day, and now you will join the ranks of those who are familiar with razors, shaving cream, depilatory creams and other methods of keeping that unwanted hair under control. But how do you know which method is right for you?

The most common method of hair removal is the old-fashioned razor and shaving cream. Many girls like it because it is quick and easy. If you're going to go this route, be sure to get a good shaving cream that has a moisturizer in it to help keep your skin soft. Only use a sharp razor, as a dull one can lead to nicks and cuts. Go slowly at first until you know how the razor feels in your hand…it's not something to rush!

A depilatory cream is another option. These creams are available in the shaving aisle at your local store. They work by dissolving the hair, so that when you wash away the cream, the hair goes with it. These creams work very well for some girls, but for others, they are a disappointment. The only way to know for sure is to give them a try! Beware if you have very sensitive skin, however – use it on just a small spot first, to make sure you don't have any breakouts from the chemicals in the cream.

There are other options for removing body hair. Many girls get their unwanted hair waxed off. You can do this at home, but be warned, it can be very painful. Some options are permanent and very expensive, like electrolysis. If you're curious about these possibilities, talk to your parents about them.

## Body Odor

Body odor is something that worries every person who goes through puberty. Everyone has body odor! There are plenty of ways to keep it under control.

Remember to take a shower every day. This might seem like a simple idea not even worth mentioning, but when you're so busy with homework and extracurricular events and friends and family, sometimes you forget to take one or simply run out of time! A good shower every day will help keep body odor in check. If you are very active, take a shower after you've worked up a good sweat.

But showers aren't enough to sufficiently control body odor. In order to do that, you need a good deodorant and antiperspirant.

Deodorants are products meant to mask or eliminate body odor. They are used under your arms, and sometimes they come in a spray to be used on other areas of your body. You can also purchase deodorant powders to keep you feeling fresh and clean.

Most deodorants are combined with an antiperspirant. Antiperspirants block the body from excessive sweating. Antiperspirants will keep your underarms dry, and that is another line of defense against body odor.

The possibilities for deodorants are mind-boggling. Most stores have a whole aisle of different choices! Look at all the labels and find one that seems right for you. There are deodorants that go on clear, so you can wear sleeveless outfits without worry. There are deodorants that come in every scent you can imagine, so you get a nice bit of perfume along with your protection. They come in roll-on, spray-on, liquid, stick, and other types.

The options are endless! But don't worry…you'll find one that is right for you.

## Body Shape and Image

Everyone comes in different shapes and sizes. It's not a matter of diet or exercise – the body shape you are born with is the one you will always have. Some people are destined to be shorter than others, while some are simply meant to be a bit curvier. The differences in everyone are what make the world a little more interesting!

You might wish you had a body like your best friend, who is turning out to be really tall. Or you might be the tall one, and wish you didn't tower over your classmates. Your hips might be a little wider than the girl who sits next to you in class, but her breasts might be smaller than the other girls. All of these things are perfectly normal. We all grow at different rates, and we all have different body shapes by the time we're finished growing.

No matter what your body type is, remember the most important part: It's YOURS. This is your body, the only one you will ever have, and it's up to you to take good care of it.

## Dieting – Why It Doesn't Work

During puberty, your body is changing into the shape you will have for the rest of your life. This is a time of enormous growth – in fact, you haven't grown this fast since you were an infant! Your body needs lots of energy to make this happen. That's why you should be kind to yourself right now, and eat all the right things your body requires to grow healthy and strong.

Dieting at this point in your life is not a good idea. Your body is still growing, and to grow properly, you need the right foods. Cutting back on calories makes your bodywork harder to do the basic things it needs to do right now. But besides that, there's a secret you need to know before you start looking at those diet books:

Dieting at this age doesn't really work!

I wouldn't blame you if you just laughed at the idea that dieting doesn't work. Everyone says it does, right? But the truth is, dieting at your age will not give you the results you think it will. Your body shape is changing, and that is genetic – there is nothing you can do to change it.

If you are a bit overweight, you can speak to your doctor about the healthiest foods to eat, but an all-out dieting binge will not help. In fact, cutting back on what you eat can lower your metabolism, and that can stop you from losing a single ounce.

The best thing to do at this point in your life is to make the healthiest choices possible. If you start with healthy choices now and stick with them, you will have no problem keeping your weight at a reasonable place. In fact, if you start with these choices now, they will become part of your lifestyle for years to come. That's the best way to treat yourself well when it comes to your eating habits!

Here are some tips to get you started:

Those colas and sports drinks have a ton of sugar in them. Do your body a favor by opting for fruit juices, water, milk, or drinks with lower sugar content.

Avoid fast food if at all possible. The food served up in the burger joints is always high in fat and cholesterol, and almost everything is fried. If you do go to a fast-food restaurant with your friends, opt for the healthier menu some places now offer, or stick with things you know are good for you, such as a grilled chicken sandwich or a side salad.

When you go to the grocery store, buy healthy snacks to munch on. Pretzels, apples, raisins, and carrots are always good choices.

Don't eat in front of the television! You will lose track of what you are eating and before you know it, that whole bag of chips is gone. Make a point of eating at the kitchen table.

Getting your vegetables every day not only helps your body grow; it also keeps you full. The fiber in the vegetables works well to keep you feeling satisfied, and so you eat less.

What other healthy ideas can you come up with? Write them down, share them with your parents, and encourage your friends to eat just as healthy as you are!

## Eating Disorders

For some people, the shock of going through puberty and dealing with all the associated changes is too much to handle. This is the time of life when eating disorders can be a real danger.

An eating disorder is an obsession with food that affects your self-image and well-being. There are two eating disorders that are much more common than any other. They are called bulimia and anorexia nervosa (anorexia for short).

Bulimia is a cycle of binging and purging. In the binging part of the cycle, someone who suffers from bulimia will eat quite a bit. Then, they will purge – meaning they will take a strong laxative or make themselves vomit to get rid of the food they just ate. Often a bulimic will avoid eating for long periods of time, then binge on foods, and purge almost immediately after they eat.

Anorexia is a disorder in which the person believes they are never thin enough. They will avoid eating at all if they can get away with it. They will also take laxatives and water pills in the hopes of losing even more weight. Sometimes they can become so thin; it is possible to see all their bones through their skin.

There are warning signs to look for when it comes to eating disorders. If you think you might have an eating disorder, take a look at the following signs. How many of them describe you?

Constant worry about your body weight.

Constantly counting calories.

Using medications to help you avoid gaining weight, such as

laxatives or water pills.

Throwing up after you eat something.

Refusing to eat even when you are ravenously hungry.

Periods that stop, or become lighter as you lose weight.

Fainting from lack of food.

Denial that there is anything wrong with you.

If you have any of these symptoms, you might have an eating disorder. This is something you need to speak with your doctor about, because you could be setting yourself up for major problems. Some common medical issues that follow eating disorders include heart problems, difficulties with kidney function, problems with your esophagus and stomach lining (from the constant throwing up) and other medical problems that can lead to massive organ failure.

In short, an eating disorder can be FATAL.

If one of your friends fits the description above, it's time to intervene. Go to a trusted adult and tell them of your concerns. Your friend might not be happy with you, but it's better to know someone is getting help than to watch him or her waste away to nothing.

Changes in your body shape are not the only thing that tells you you're growing up. There are other signs that you are on the threshold of adulthood.

## Getting Your Period

This is the biggest sign of all that you are on your way to becoming an adult. Starting your period is a rite of passage for every girl, and it's something that you can look forward to with both dread and anticipation.

The timetable might be a bit different for every girl – some girls start their periods at a very young age, while others might be sixteen or even older before they see the first signs of menstruation. When you do get your period, it might come every month at first, or it might not...it could take a while for your body to decide what is best for it, and to settle into somewhat of a schedule.

Getting your period means your body is growing normally. It means you are maturing just as you should be. It might also be a very emotional time for you, because it means your days of childhood are coming to a close. That can be a difficult thing for anyone to face, and if you feel a little depressed or weepy during those few weeks after you start your period, it's okay. Many girls do feel that way.

You will have a lot of questions about your period and what it all means.

## What is Really Happening?

The medical term for your period is menstruation. There are many names for it, most of them handed down from one generation to another. "Aunt Flo" or "The Monthly Visit" are two common terms for the time during the month when you menstruate.

Menstruation marks a major change in your body. It means

you are growing up. Your body has been preparing itself all this time, and now that you have started your period, life has just handed you a major responsibility. As girls grow and change, nature's plan is to make sure you can procreate. Your period is a sign that your body is mature enough to get pregnant.

But what is *really* happening? Here's how your body works and why you have your period every month:

You were born with two ovaries in your body. Your ovaries are tiny little sacs in your lower abdomen. They are attached to fallopian tubes. These tubes are very tiny! The tubes attach to your uterus. You are born with all of these body parts inside you, and they never give you a moment of trouble. In fact, you are completely unaware of them until you hit puberty.

Each ovary holds thousands of eggs. Hard to believe that there could be thousands of eggs inside you, isn't it? When you go through puberty, your body starts getting ready to release those eggs. They are usually released from your ovaries one at a time. When they are released, they travel down the fallopian tubes and wind up in your uterus.

You don't feel any of this! It is all happening inside you, naturally, just like your heart beating. It is something that happens, but that you don't notice and probably rarely think about.

Before the egg is released, your body spends several weeks building up a "lining" in your uterus. This lining has been built with extra blood and tissues from your body. When the egg is finally released and it travels to your uterus, it winds up in that lining. If you have sex during this time and the egg gets fertilized by the male sperm, it settles into the lining and uses the extra blood and tissue to help it grow during those first few weeks.

But if you don't get pregnant, then you have your period. Your body has to get rid of the uterine lining in order to start the process all over again. Your body gets rid of that uterine lining by tiny contractions that push the lining out of you. This flow of blood and bits of tissue is known as your period.

You will have your period for anywhere from three to seven days. Most girls are on the average, and have their period for around four or five days. The blood you see during your period can be many different shades of red. Sometimes it's so dark it looks almost brown, and other times it is a brighter red. Sometimes the blood will have what looks like tiny solid pieces in it. These are usually referred to as "clots" and they are nothing to worry about.

You might pass just a little bit of blood and be done – or you might pass a lot for three or four days. Just as with everything else during puberty, the amount of blood varies from one person to another.

When your period is over, your body starts the whole process over again.

**What it means**

You might not have given sex a passing thought at this point, but once you begin your period, you need to be aware of what it really means. If you do have sexual intercourse with someone, you could become pregnant. That is a huge responsibility! It is wonderful to know your body is working properly, but it's also important that you understand exactly what your body can do.

That's why it's so important to talk to someone you trust when you start your period. Your parents are the first choice, but if you don't feel comfortable with asking them questions, visit a school counselor or another trusted adult who can give you some answers.

Before you start your period, you will probably be thinking about it already, and wondering when the first period will arrive. For peace of mind, make some plans! It's impossible to know when your period will start, but you can be prepared when it does come.

**Emergency kit**

To be ready for the moment when your period does arrive, plan ahead with a Period Emergency Kit. This kit is very easy to put together and will give you the peace of mind you need.

Start by choosing a small container, such as makeup bag or tiny purse. It needs to be something you can put in the bottom of your backpack or tuck away into the back of your locker. Make sure it is big enough to hold the supplies you will need.

If you use pads, make sure to put a few of those in the bag. If you use tampons, put a few of those in there, too. Also put an extra pair of underwear, as well as a washcloth for cleanup if you do have a little bit of a mess to tend to in the bathroom. You might want to slip a few plastic sandwich bags in there as well, just in case your bathroom at school doesn't have a private disposal in the stall. You will use those bags to wrap soiled underwear or used pads for disposal.

Some people also put a few dollars in coins in the bag, just in case you run out of supplies and have to buy more from a vending machine in the bathroom. Some schools have those vending machines and some don't – if you are in a place that doesn't offer the machines, make sure to tuck some extra supplies into your bag.

You can make more than one of these bags. You can put one in the back of your locker, one in your backpack, and one in the glove compartment of your family vehicle. You can even make them for your friends…make it a slumber party project!

Having peace of mind about your supplies will help you relax about your period. It's always good to know you're prepared, and it takes the anxiety out of the question of what to do if you start your period unexpectedly.

**Using Your Supplies**

When you start your period, there are several options for taking care of the flow. What you do to handle your period is a very personal choice. It is also something you are going to deal with for the majority of your life, so don't hesitate to try different methods to find the one that best suits you!

Most girls start out with pads. Maxi pads are the long, padded strips that have adhesive on the back. The adhesive presses against the inside of your panties and holds the pad in place. The first time you wear a pad, it will probably feel rather bulky, or even a bit uncomfortable until you get used to it. You will need to change your pad every few hours to make sure you have enough protection to capture all the blood associated with your period.

Tampons are another option that many girls love. Tampons are a bit harder to use than pads, but they provide protection on the inside, rather than the outside. Many girls like the freedom that tampons can give you – for instance, if you have chosen the right tampon, you can even go swimming and no one will ever know you're on your period!

Okay, but how do they work? Tampons work by expanding as they soak up the fluids of your period. As they expand, they press against the walls of your vaginal canal. You don't feel it when this happens, but the tampon is blocking the flow of blood and instead of letting it out of your body, it is soaking it up into the fabric of the tampon.

Tampons can be a bit daunting at first. Be patient the first time you use one, and give yourself plenty of time to read all the information that comes along with the tampons. Putting a tampon in is a very simple process, and taking it out is even easier.

There are other options to handle your period, but none of them are as popular as the methods we've already talked about.

## Some Common Period Fears

Everyone has questions about what might happen during their period. Here is a list of common fears all girls your age have at one time or another, and what to do about them.

### What if you get blood on your clothes?

This happens to every woman at one time or another, and it's an annoyance. If you do find blood on your clothes, change immediately, and be sure to change your pad or tampon. If you can't change, swing your skirt around so the bloodstain is at the side or if you have a jumper, tie it around your waist and let it hang to cover the blood.

The blood in your clothes can be removed if you move quickly and use the right methods!

Follow these easy instructions to take care of the problem:

Keep in mind that a fresh stain is much easier to clean than a dried one. If you can wash out the blood immediately, then you have a much better chance of making things easier on yourself!

If the item is color-safe, you can try hydrogen peroxide. Simply pour the hydrogen peroxide on the spot, let it bubble away, and check the fabric after the foaming stops. If there is still a bit of stain there, use more hydrogen peroxide. This usually works very well. Once the stain is gone, wash and dry as usual.

If the blood happens to be on something white, you're in luck – bleach will do the trick quite well. Simply use watered-down bleach on the spot, and then wash the item as usual, adding a bit of bleach to the water. The stain will be gone in no time!

Never, ever put hot water on a bloodstain. If you do this, it will set into the fabric and even the hydrogen peroxide might not get it out. Also, if there is any bit of the stain left, don't put the item in the dryer. The blood will turn brown when heat is applied, and nothing will be able to remove it.

If nothing else works, there's always the dry cleaners. They might be able to help!

**Can the tampon get stuck?**

Each tampon comes with a long string woven into the center. This string is what you gently tug on when it's time to take the tampon out.

Tampons can't get "stuck" but they can get "lost." If you reach down for the string and don't feel it at first, don't panic! That little string can get moved around by the usual motion of your body, and it sometimes might take a moment to find it. Once you find it, simply pull the tampon out.

The warning that the tampon can get lost inside your body and wind up in your abdomen is a MYTH. This cannot happen. Why? The blood of your menstrual period flows out through your cervix. Your cervix is a small, hard area at the top of your vagina. It is open very little, just enough to allow your menstrual fluids to pass through. There is no way a tampon could make its way up there.

**Will I faint from loss of blood?**

No. The blood you lose during your period is a natural amount, what your body is supposed to lose. This blood has been built up for weeks along your uterine lining, so it's not coming from your normal blood supply. It's simply sloughing off and leaving your body. The process doesn't result in major blood loss, and you will not faint because of it.

## But it looks like a lot...

When you have your period, it can look like quite a bit of blood is coming out of you. Some women have very heavy periods, and those can be the scariest of all! But you are not losing any more blood than your body is meant to lose. If you are still concerned about how much blood you are losing, mention your concerns to your doctor and get the reassurance you need.

## Toxic Shock Syndrome

When you open up that box of tampons, you will probably notice a printed box filled with all kinds of dire warnings. Manufacturers of tampons are required to put notices on the boxes about something called Toxic Shock Syndrome. It sounds scary, but it's very rare.

Toxic Shock Syndrome is an illness caused by a buildup of bacteria and toxins in the body. The immune system can't fight off the problem, and TSS is the result. The problem is often linked to tampon use, mostly because the earliest cases of the illness were linked to superabsorbent tampons, especially those that didn't have to be changed as often.

Keep in mind that not all TSS cases are caused by tampons. In fact, only about half of them are. Other cases can be triggered by bacteria in a wound, such as an open sore or a cut that hasn't yet healed. But it is important to know what TSS is and the steps to take to make your slight risk even slighter.

There are very clear signs when you have TSS. These signs happen suddenly, and can include the following:

Very high fever (greater than 102 Fahrenheit)

A rash over your entire body that looks much like sunburn

Vomiting, nausea, and diarrhea

Severe muscle aches, weakness, and fatigue

Headache, sometimes accompanied by confusion or disorientation

Feeling lightheaded or fainting, usually the result of a rapid drop in blood pressure

If you are one of the very few who does get TSS, it is a very serious situation. If you suspect this is happening to you, take out the tampon you have in and go straight to the doctor or hospital.

It sounds very scary, and it is. But your risks of getting TSS are very, very low. You can make sure those risks STAY low by keeping the following tips in mind:

If you have a wound on your body, keep it clean and covered with a bandage

If you have any signs of infection on your body, such as a wound that is red or swollen, call your doctor about it right away

If you use tampons, use the ones with the absorbency you need, and change them every few hours. If you are hanging out at home, try using pads instead.

TSS is a very rare and serious illness. However, if you know the signs and can recognize them quickly, your odds of long-term problems from TSS are very small.

**Period Cramps and Pain**

Remember the explanation about what really happens during your period? If you don't get pregnant, your body gets rid of the uterine lining, and that's what your period is. But how does your body do this, exactly? It gets rid of the lining through a small series of contractions designed to push the uterine lining out of your body. Those small contractions might sometimes be felt as cramping. You might feel the cramps in one single spot or throughout your whole abdomen. These cramps are usually just a bit uncomfortable, but for some young women, they can feel a little worse than that.

That's when it's time to take something to alleviate the discomfort. It is just like getting rid of a headache – there are natural remedies to deal with it, and there are over the counter options as well. Try the natural remedies first, and if those don't work, talk with your doctor about medications that will work well for you.

**Natural Remedies**

Sometimes, rest is the best natural remedy you can imagine. Curl up on the couch with a good book and a comfortable pillow. Press another pillow against your lower belly. The pressure of the pillow can make your cramps lessen.

If you prefer something more, try a hot water bottle. They are old-fashioned and quaint, but they have been around forever for a very good reason – they WORK! Fill the bottle with warm water and press it against your abdomen to get some relief from the aches.

Some women swear by different hot teas during their period to lessen the discomfort. Specifically, rose tea, ginger tea or oregano tea have been shown to help.

Exercise helps. It might seem counter-productive – after all, you're hurting, so why would you want to push your body into exercise of any kind? – but studies have shown that regular exercise can reduce cramps or even eliminate them altogether. Yoga has also been reported as a fantastic pain reliever during your period.

**Over the Counter**

If you have tried the natural remedies but they don't provide enough relief, using an over-the-counter medication might be your best bet. There are medications like Ibuprofen that can help with the aches (you must always take these medications after eating food). Other medications, such as Midol or Ponstan (different countries name these painkillers different names) are formulated to help with the cramps, possible headaches and bloating that can be associated with your period. Try out a few of them until you find the one that works for your symptoms. You may need to visit your doctor if these medications and natural remedies don't relieve your cramps and pains.

## Boyfriends

When your body starts to change, you aren't the only one who notices. Boys suddenly begin to notice you more than ever before. The guys who teased you a few years ago are now falling all over themselves to spend time with you. They are paying attention to your every word! How did this happen…and what in the world are you supposed to do about it?

The sudden attention from boys might leave you feeling a little lost. Even your friends who just happened to be boys now seem to see you differently, and that can lead to some hurt feelings. But it can also lead to some wonderful, heady happiness, because all these boys are noticing you!

The best thing to do is continue to treat everyone the way you did before. Be kind and polite to everyone. If a boy asks you out on a date, talk to your parents about it. They might not want you to date at this age. Instead of being girlfriends with one particular boy, why not make a point of staying in big groups? That way you always have someone to hang out with, and you get to know everybody better.

If you do find yourself attracted to one particular boy, it's time to take your parents into confidence. If they aren't ready to hear what you have to say about your romantic feelings, then you should talk to someone else, perhaps a guidance counselor or older sibling who understands what you are going through.

There will come a time when you do find yourself spending more time with one particular boy. Think carefully about what being a girlfriend means! It means you are making a commitment to spend your time with that particular boy, and you aren't going to be dating or "going steady" with anyone else. That's a pretty big deal, especially when you're so young.

Your parents need to know about the boy you are interested in, and they need to have a chance to meet him and learn a bit more about him. Don't hide your boyfriend from your family! If you do, they will think you don't want them to know about him…and that can lead them to question why. Trust is very important, so always be open about your feelings for your boyfriend, and make sure your family understands what you are thinking.

## A Final Word

This is a very important time in your life. Learn all you can about the changes and then…relax! Enjoy these years. They might seem tough to get through, but one day you will look back and see a whole new you. You have to go through the changes today to find that beautiful, wonderful person you will become tomorrow!

Enjoy the journey young ladies!

*Karen and Katrina*

Authors, Speakers, Educational and Parenting Experts

**P.s.** *Thank you for reading our book. If you liked it, could we please ask you to leave a rating and a comment and tell your friends about it.*

*You may also enjoy reading our book –*

*How to Make Friends and Be Popular...*

*Have you read Julia Jones Diary?*

*Book 1 is FREE! Try it out...*

*You can also follow us on Instagram*

*@juliajonesdiary*

*and Facebook*

*www.facebook.com/JuliaJonesDiary*

Made in the USA
San Bernardino, CA
17 September 2017